Our Fragile World

30 postcards

Reprinted 2006

www.newint.org
Design by Ian Nixon/New Internationalist

British Library Cataloguing-in-Publication Data.
A catalogue record for this book is available from the British Library.

ISBN 1 904456 26 X

Printed on recycled card by C & C Offset Printing Co. Ltd., China,
who hold the environmental accreditation ISO 14001

To accompany the book *Our Fragile World – the beauty of a planet under pressure*
by Troth Wells and Caspar Henderson

Our Fragile World

The 21st century may see faster and more dramatic change to the world's ecosystems in the course of just a few decades than has occurred for tens or in some cases hundreds of thousands of years. In a world that also supports six billion human beings, going on ten billion by mid-century, the changes are likely to make the world a much more dangerous place.

The biggest threats to ecosystems include war, climate change and global warming leading to melting glaciers, rising sea levels, drought and fires as well as species loss, from tigers to coral reefs. But all is not yet lost.

The human capacity to adapt, to learn to live within limits, to design sustainable systems, and to restore ecosystems that seemed lost should not be underestimated.

This collection of wonderful images from some of the world's top photographers – including many sponsored by the UN's Environment Programme – shows the remarkable loveliness of the world. See the orange glory of the Namib desert, the astonishing green-and-red of a tree frog, the extraordinary detail of a starfish; children dancing; the charm of baby elephants and penguins; ancient rice terraces or the destructive but awesome power of lava setting fire to a tree.

This book of postcards accompanies the NI book *Our Fragile World – the beauty of a planet under pressure* by Troth Wells and Caspar Henderson; for details please turn to the back of this book or visit our website **www.newint.org**

'Extraordinary pictures...showing the beauty and fragility of the world around us – and exactly what we stand to lose if we fail.'

Dr Caroline Lucas, Green Party MEP

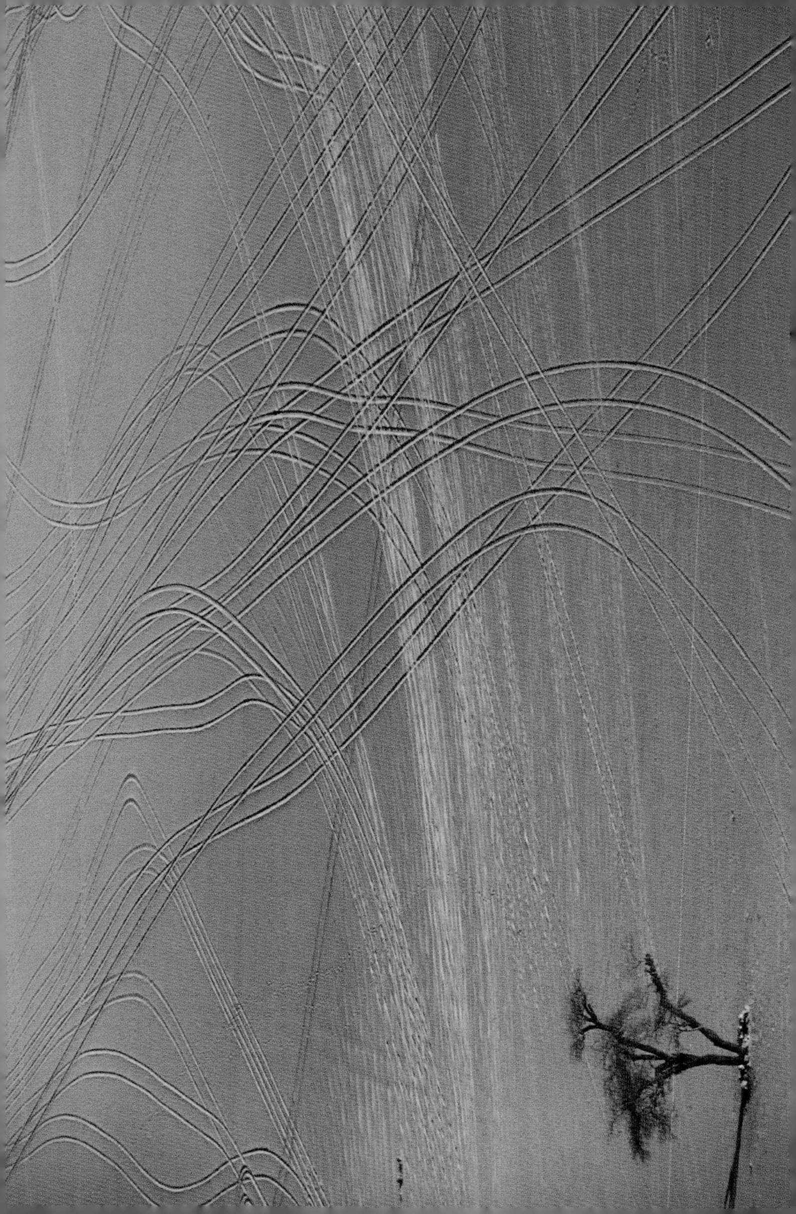

Tassili desert, Algeria *Dieter Telemans/Panos*

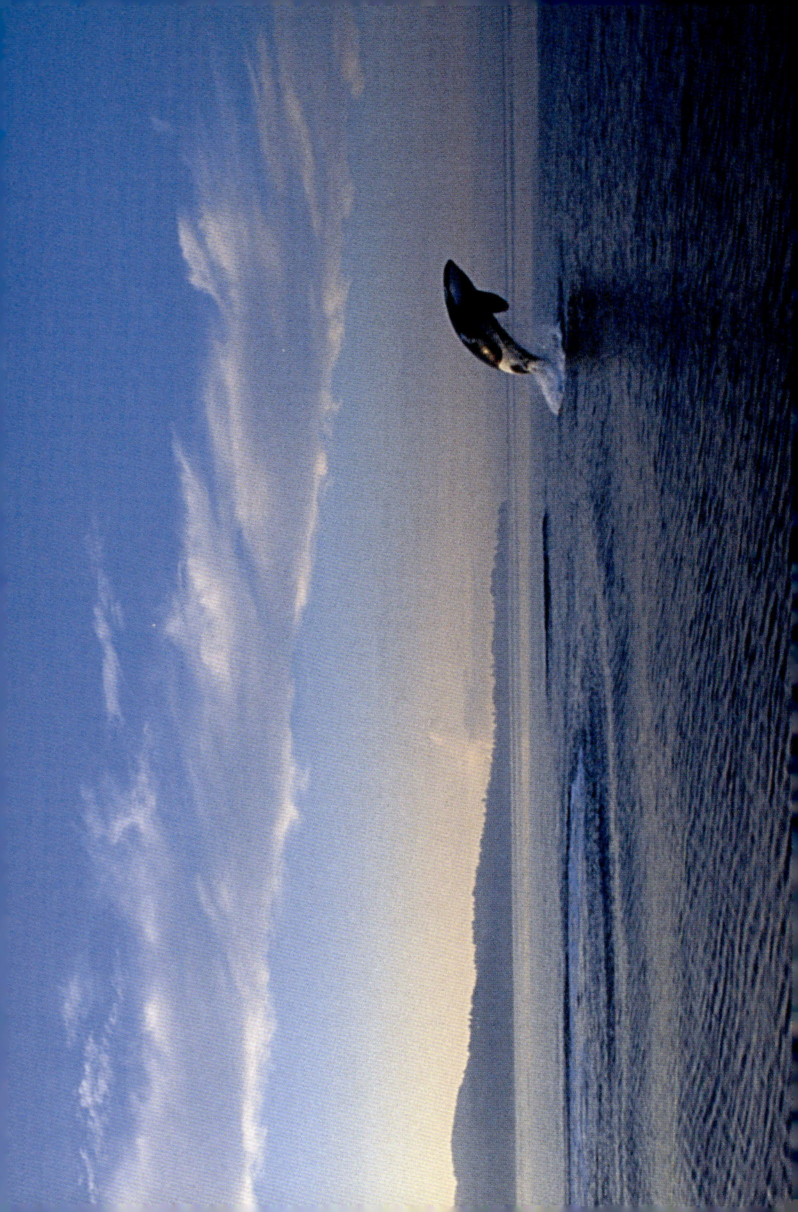

Orca ('killer whale'), Washington, USA *Ray Pfortner/Still Pictures*

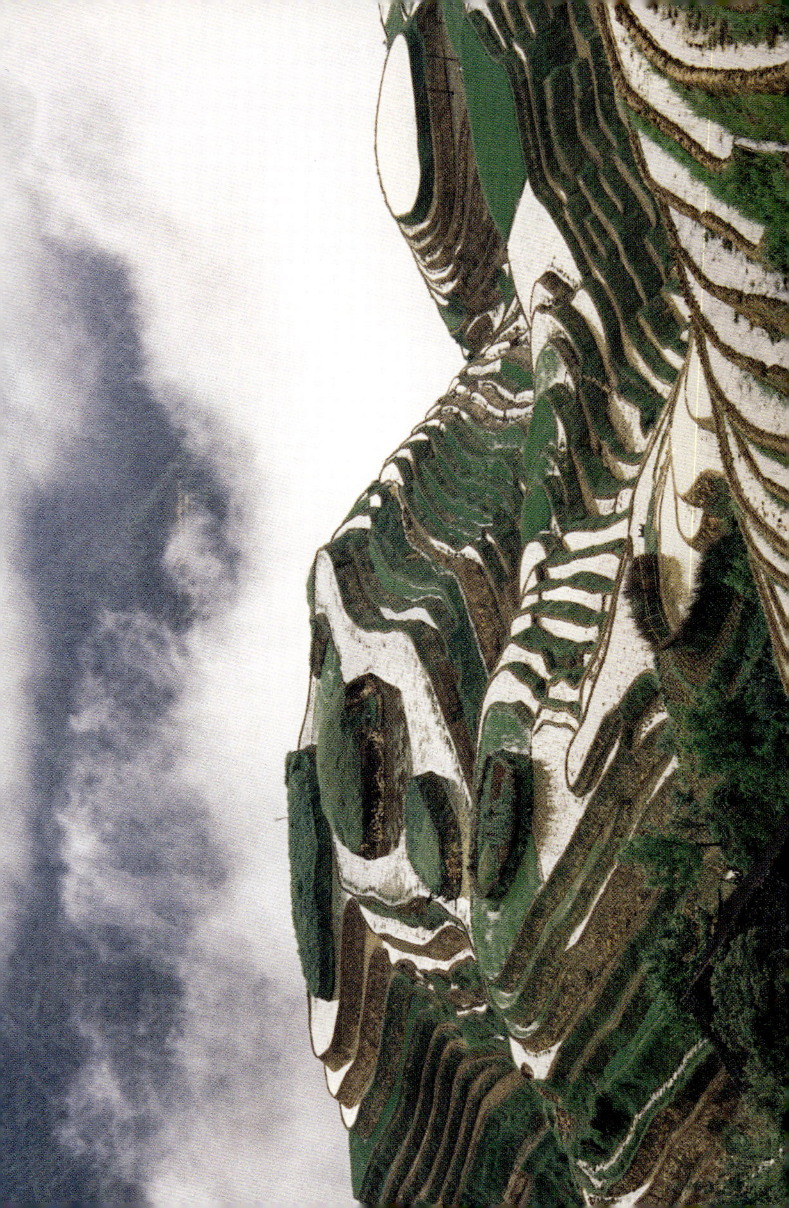

Rice terraces, Guangxi, China *Xintian Pan/UNEP/Still Pictures*

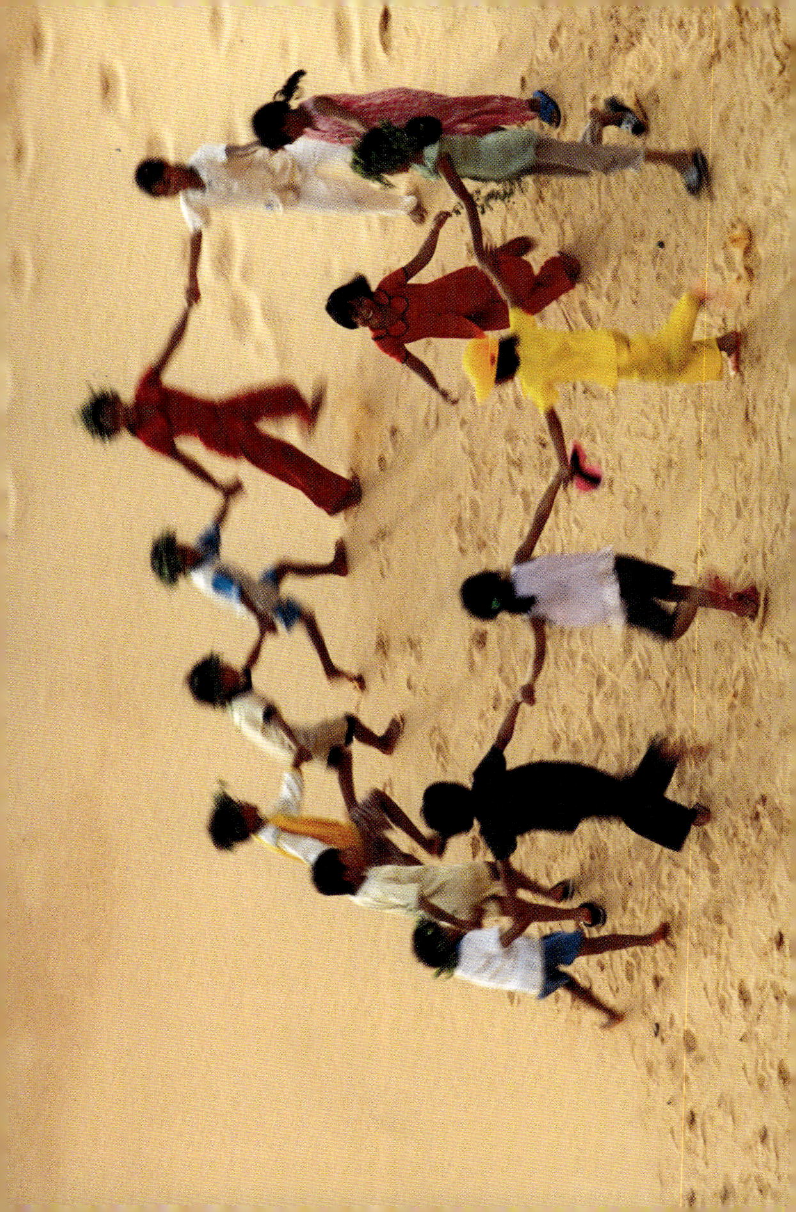

Children, Vietnam *Tran Cao Bao Long/UNEP/Still Pictures*

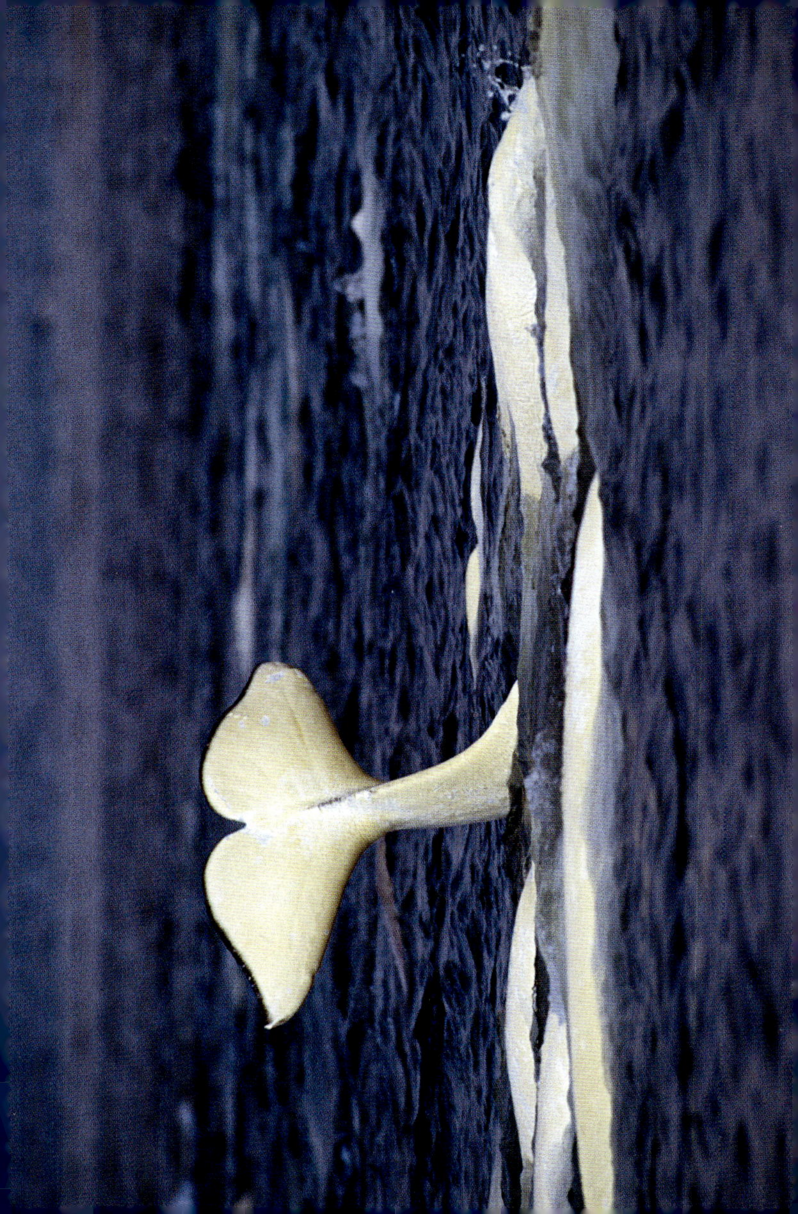

Beluga whales, Canada *Günter Ziesler/Still Pictures*

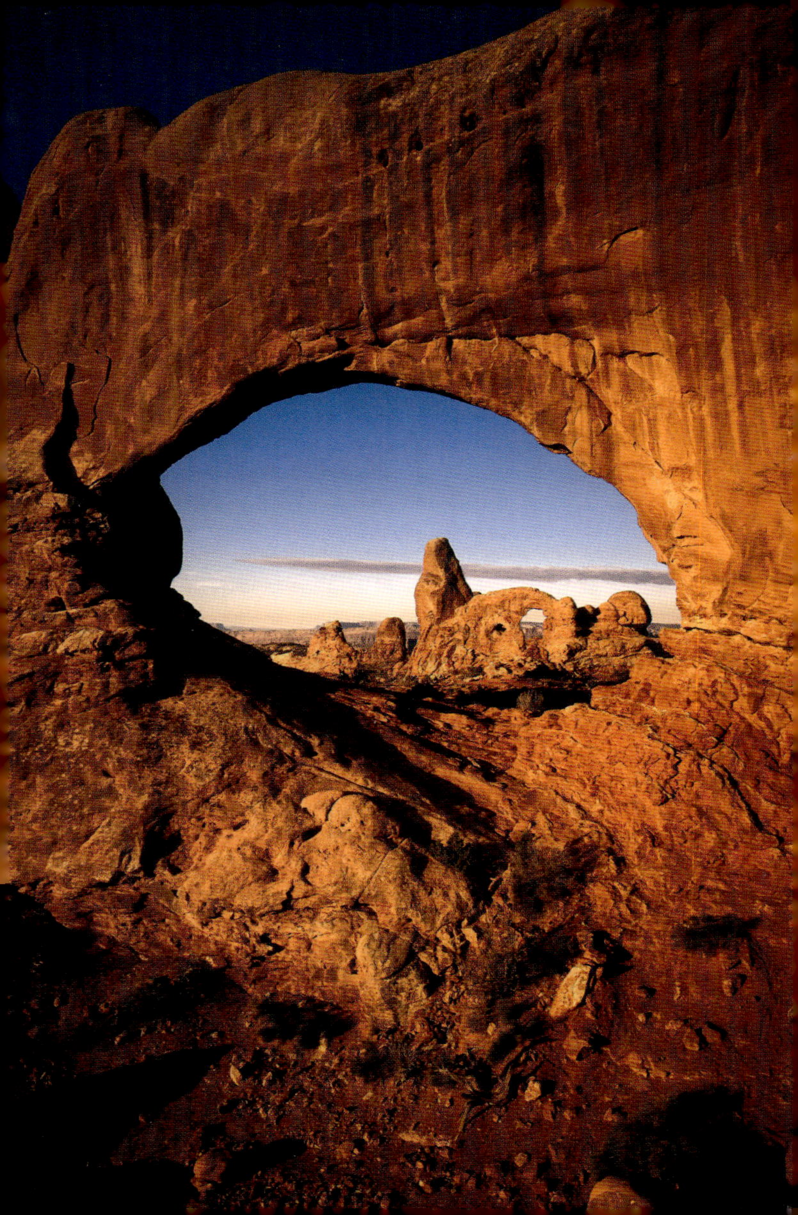

Turret Arch, Utah, USA *Keith Kent/Still Pictures*

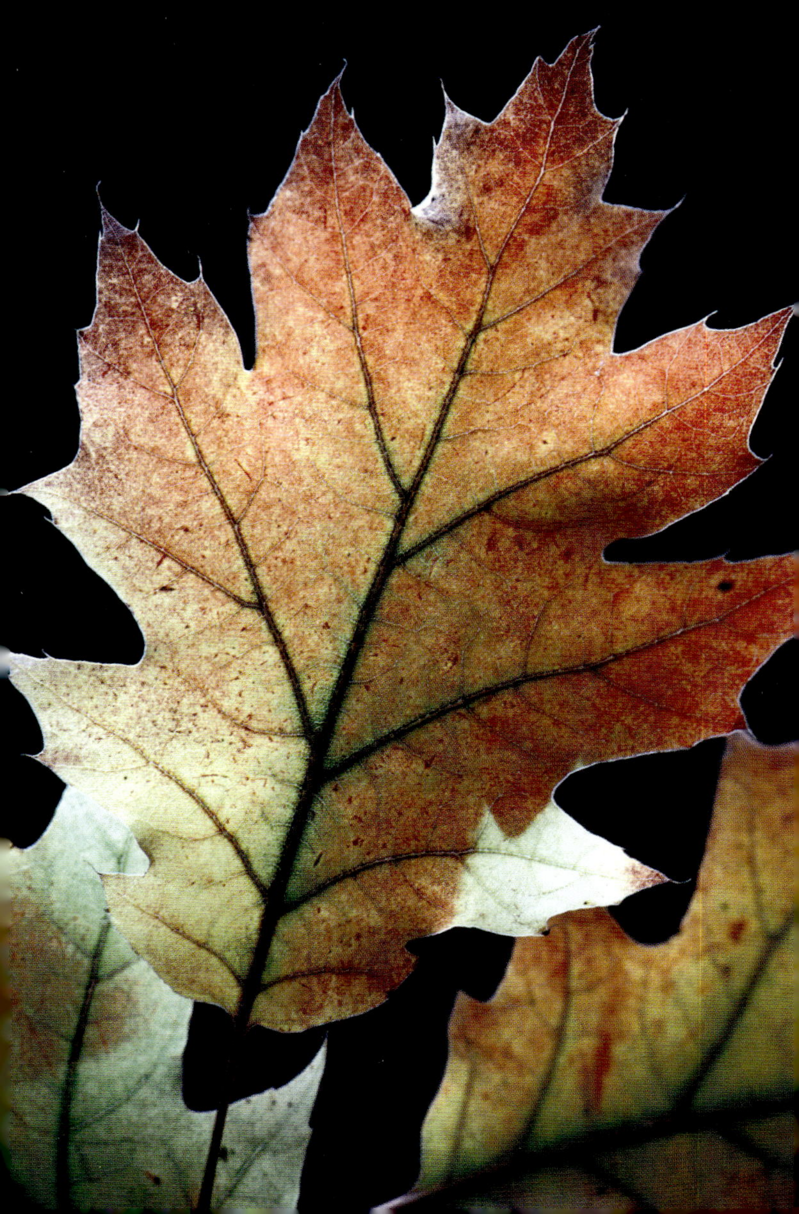

Oak leaves, Germany *A Riedmiller/Still Pictures*

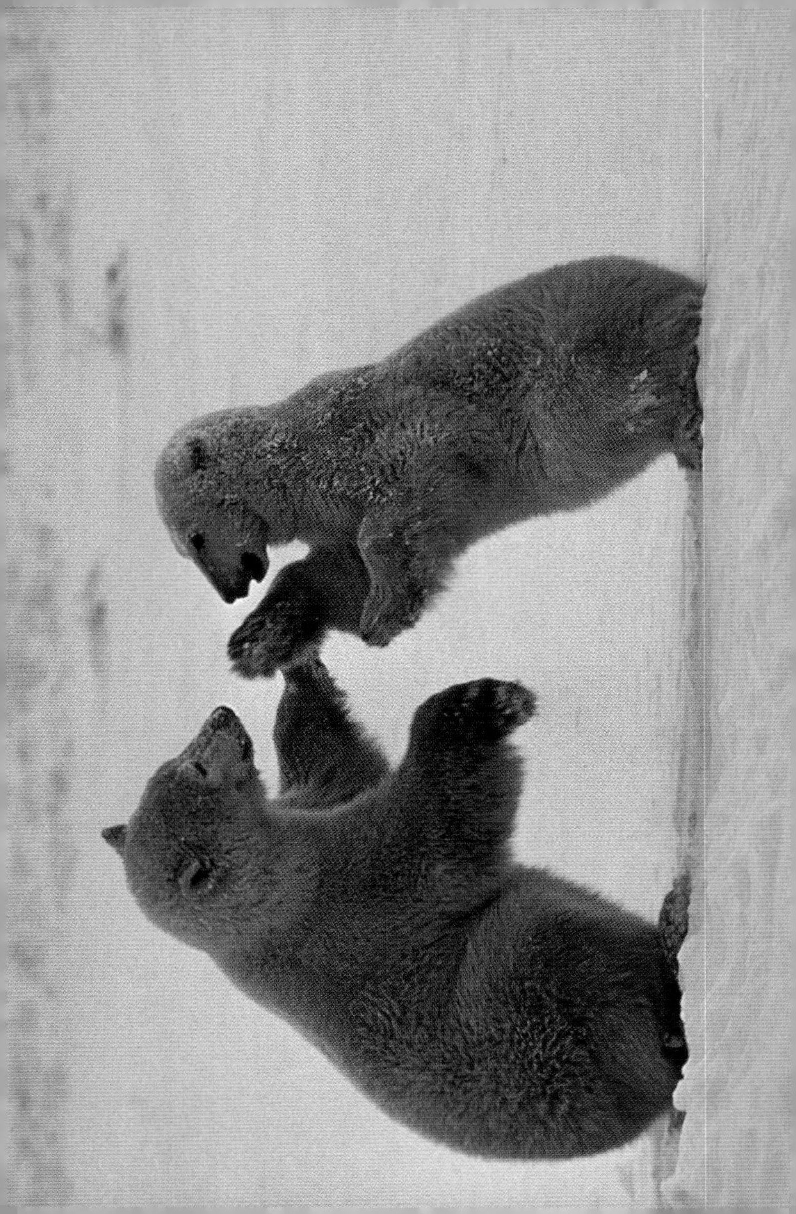

Polar bears, Arctic *SJ Krasemann/Still Pictures*

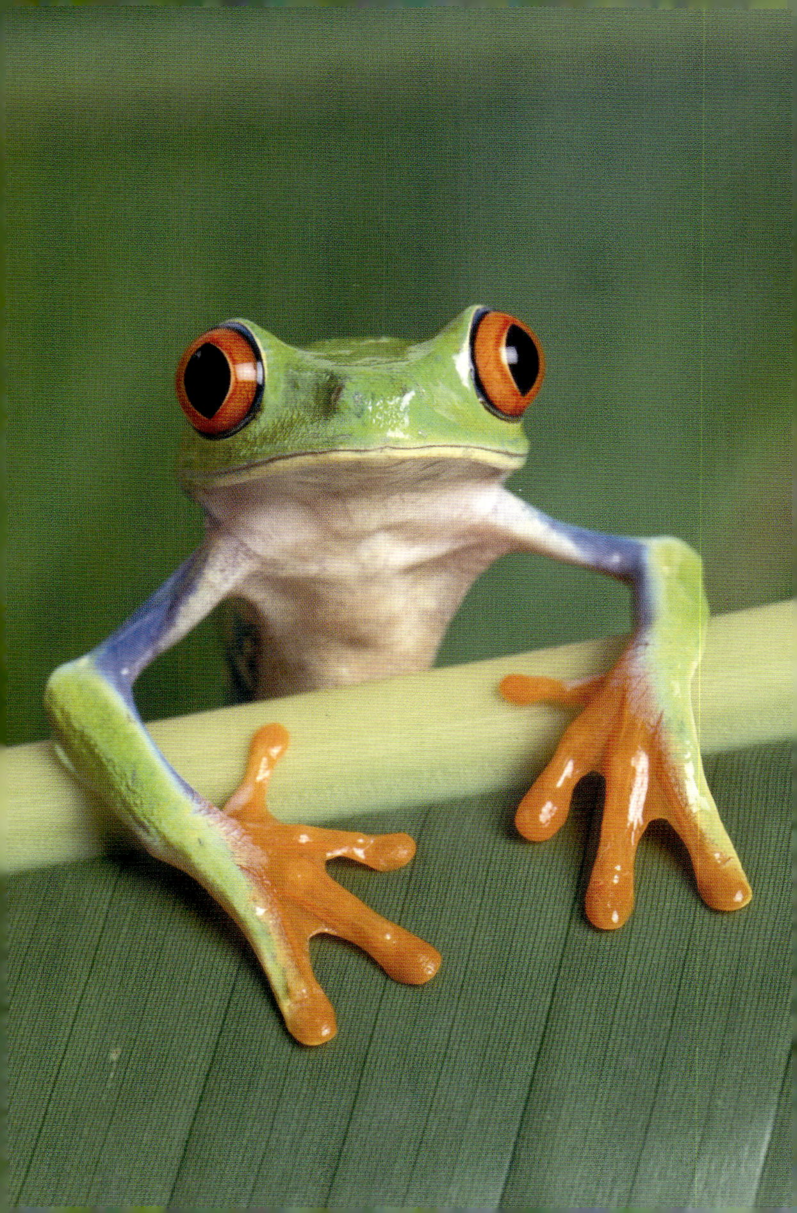

Red-eyed tree frog *Klein/Still Pictures*

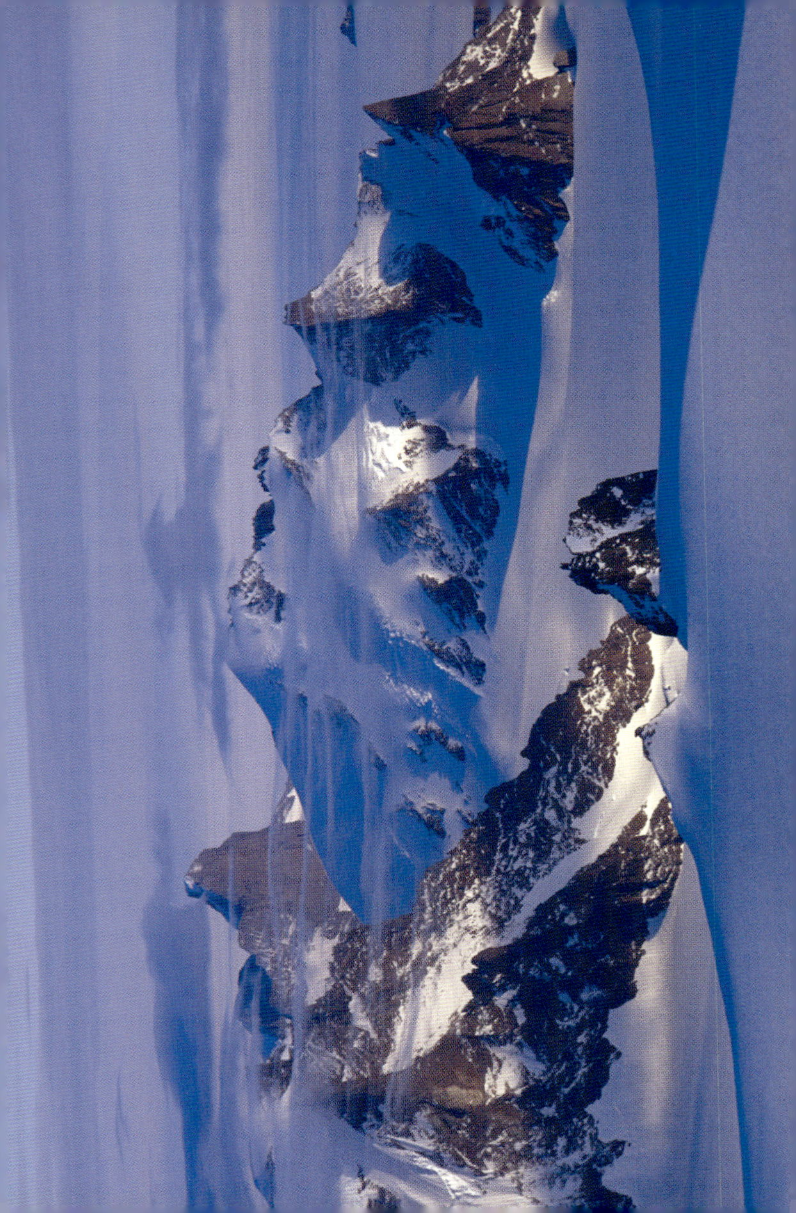

Antarctica, Queen Maud Land *Gordon Wiltsie/Still Pictures*

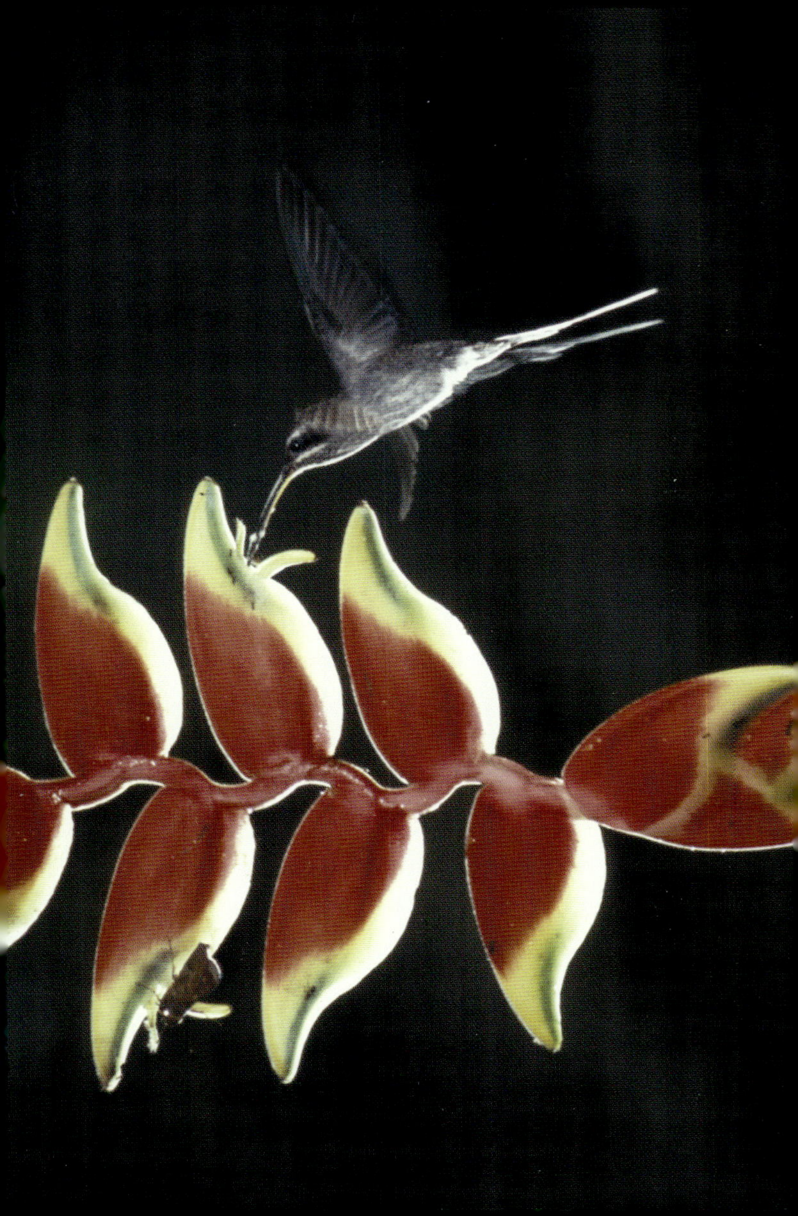

Hummingbird, Peru *Günter Ziesler/Still Pictures*

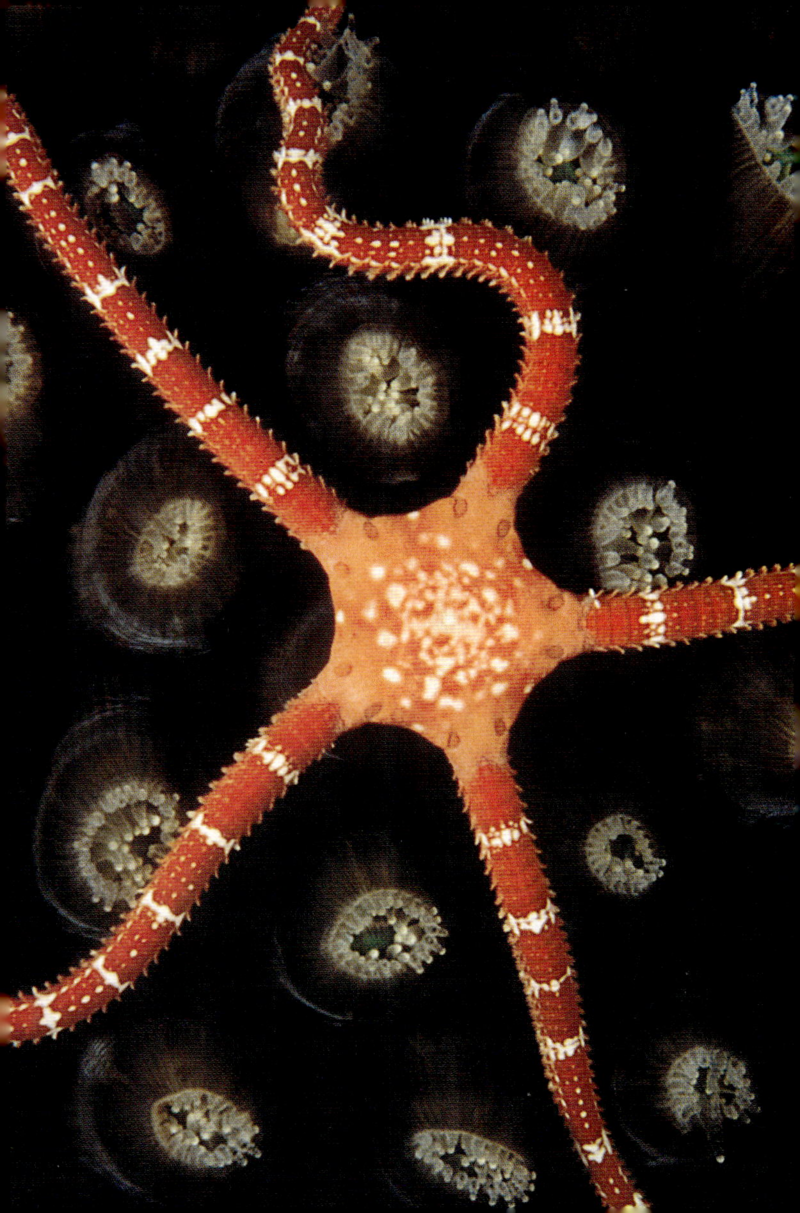

Ruby Brittle Starfish, Bahamas *J Croop/UNEP/Still Pictures*

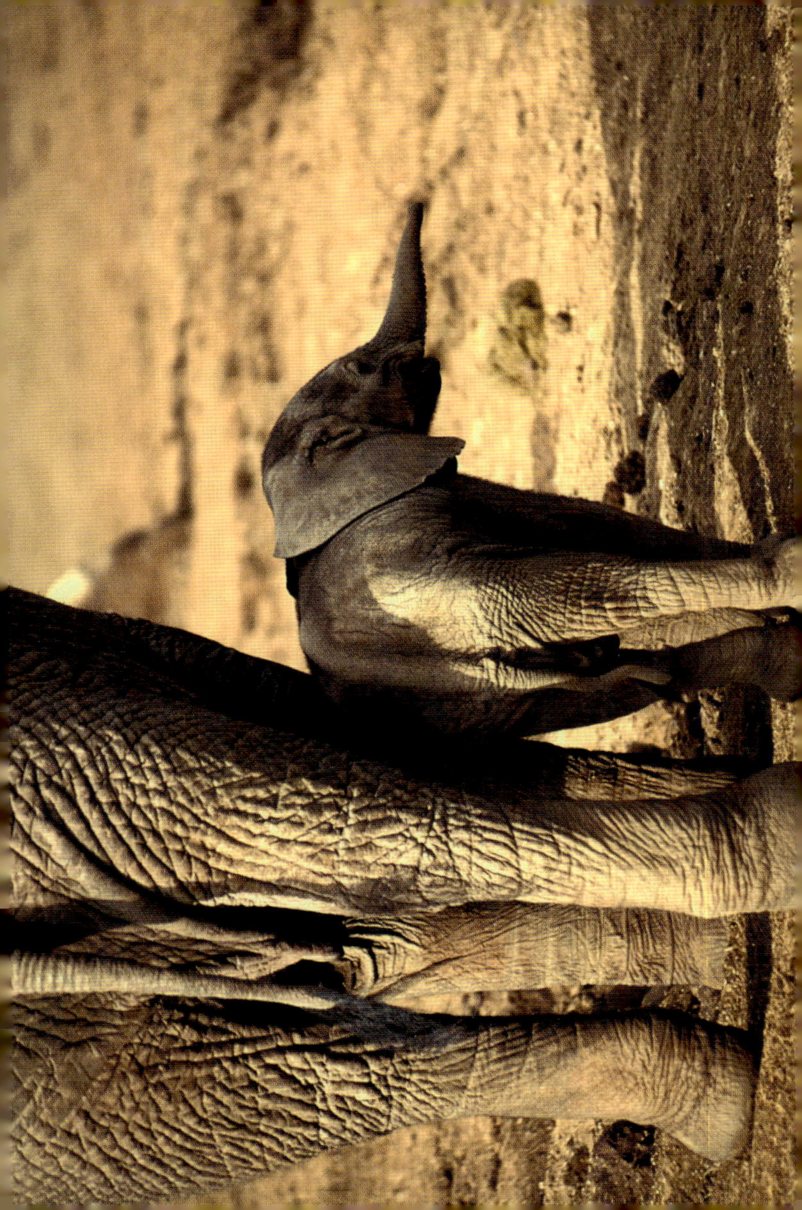

Elephants, Kenya *Charlotte Thege/Still Pictures*

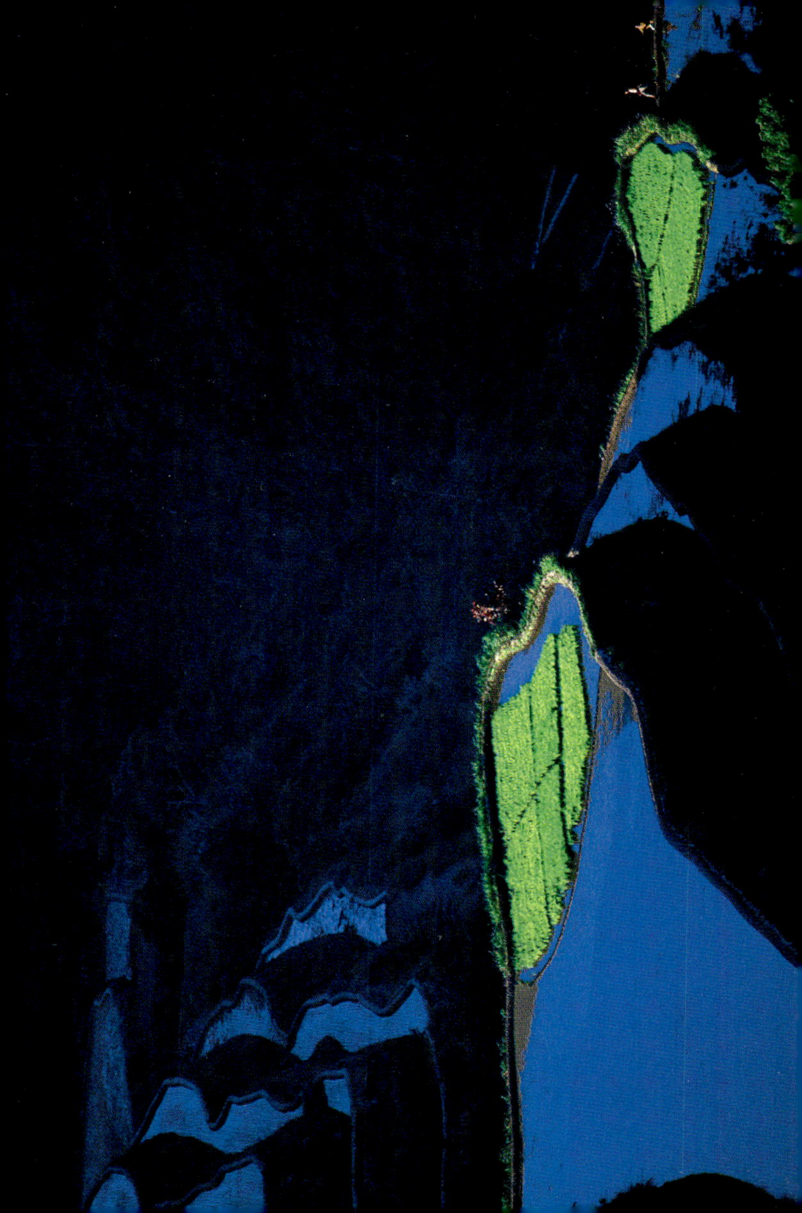

Banaue rice terraces, Philippines *Chris Stowers/Panos*

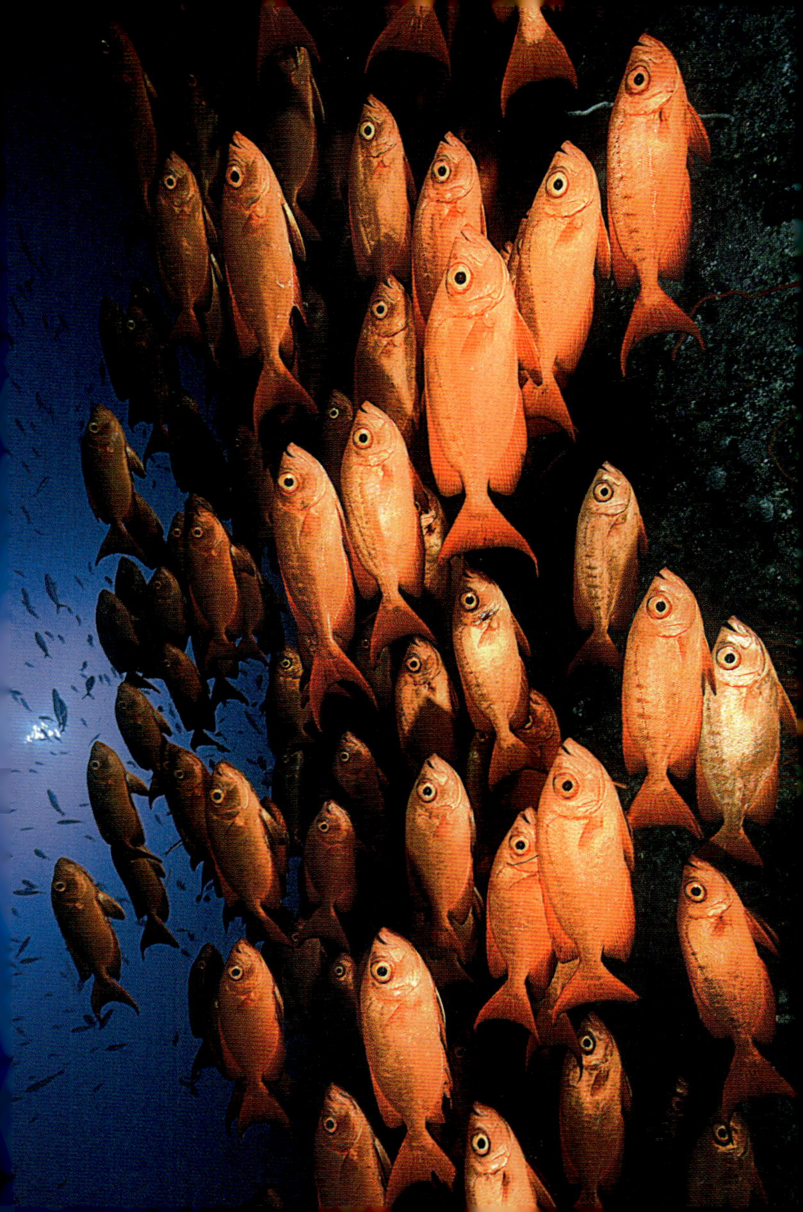

Crescent-tail bigeyes, Great Barrier Reef, Australia *Fred Bavendam/Still Pictures*

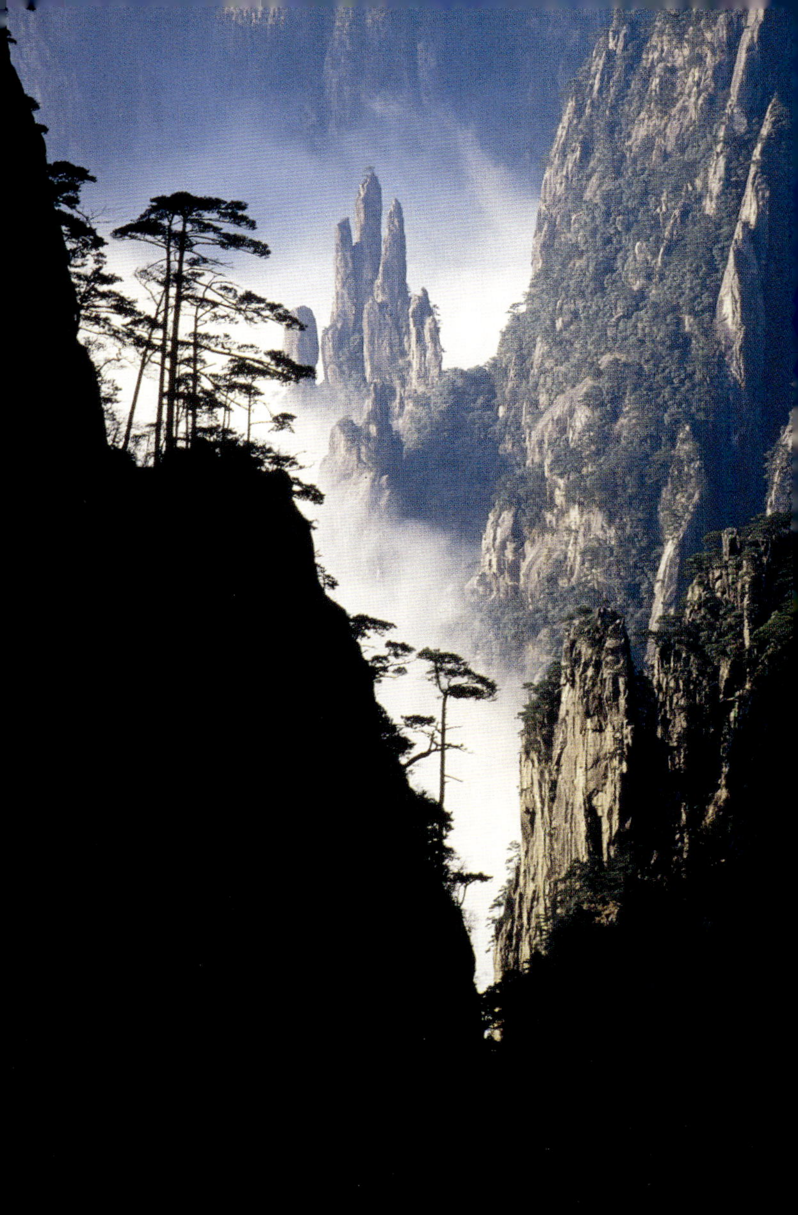

Site of Three Gorges Dam, China *D Stanfill/UNEP/Still Pictures*

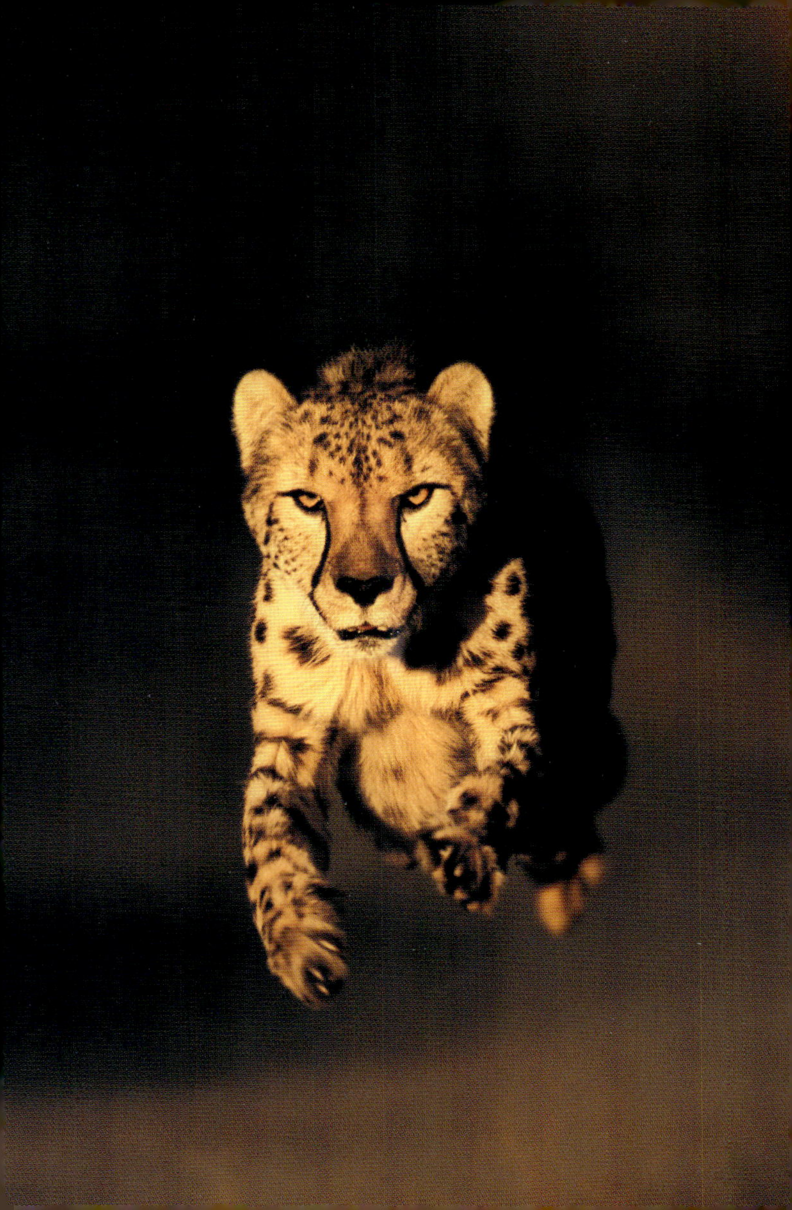

Cheetah *Martin Harvey/Still Pictures*

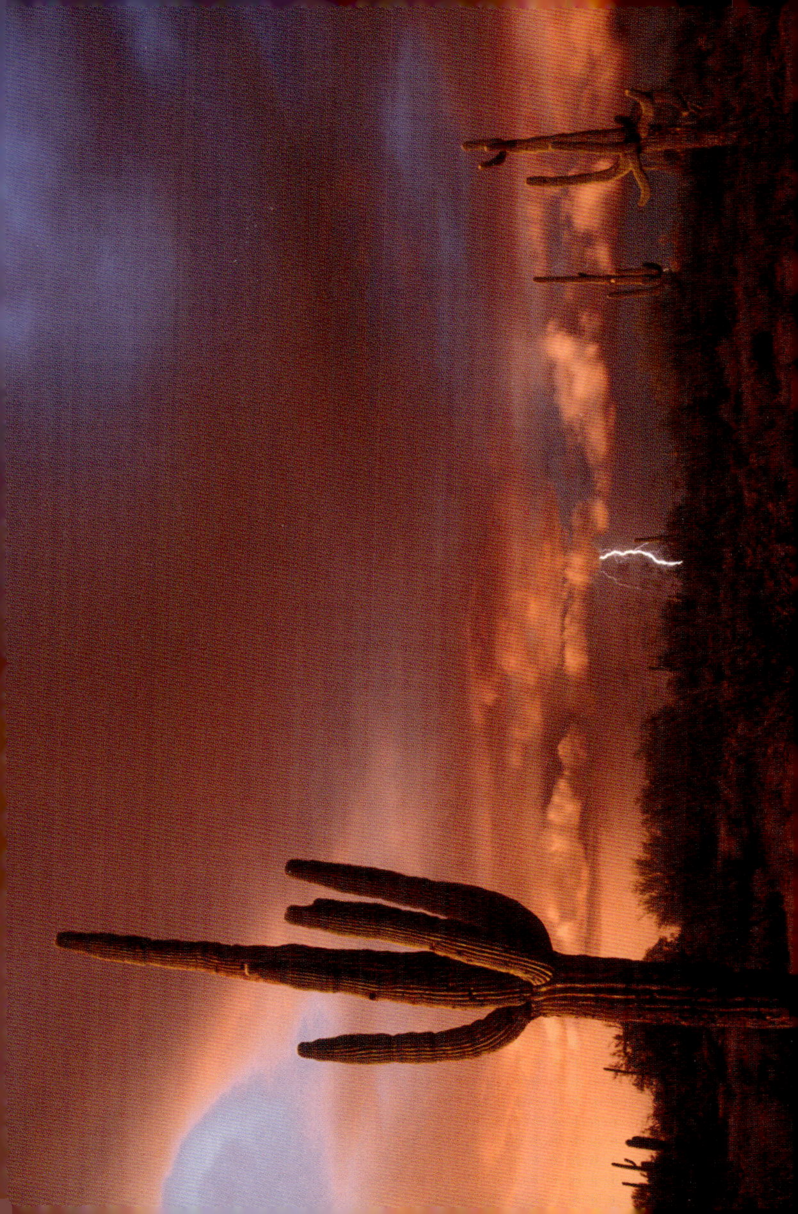

Approaching storm, Arizona, USA *Gene Rhoden/Still Pictures*

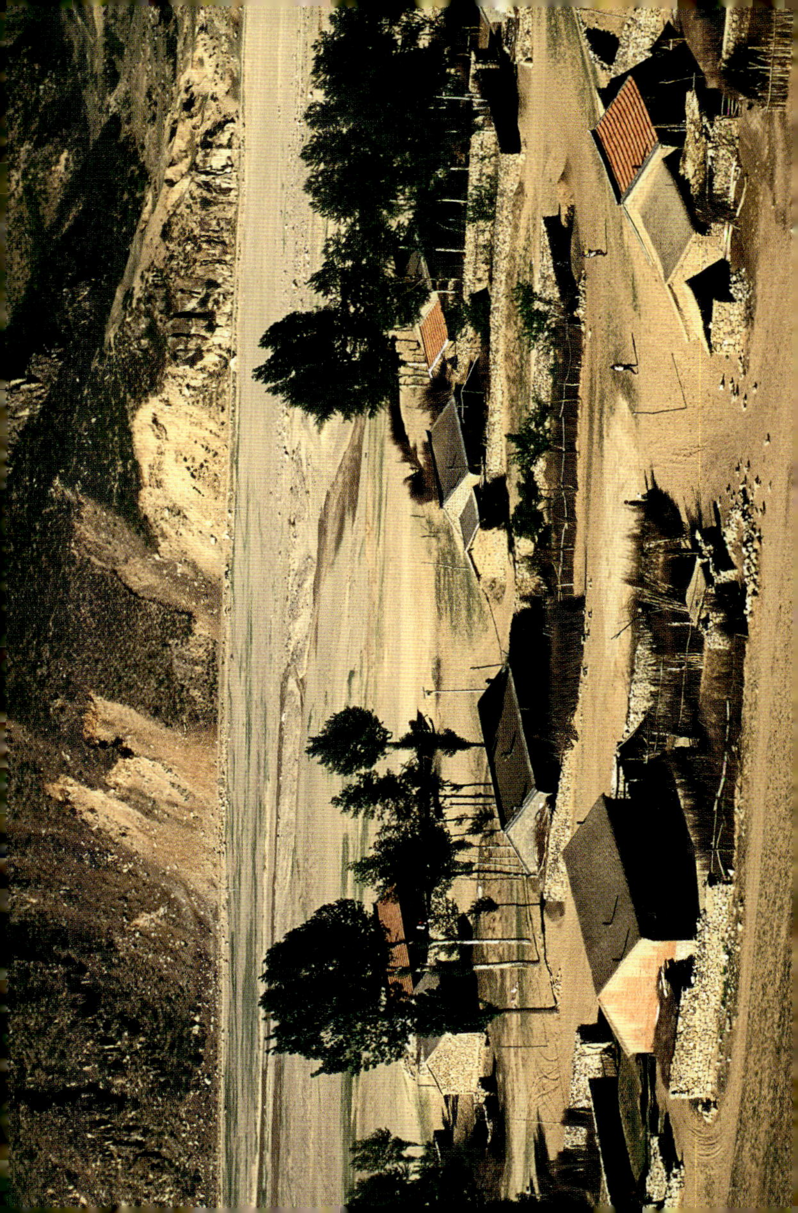

Desertification in Langtou Gou, China *Mark Henley/Panos*

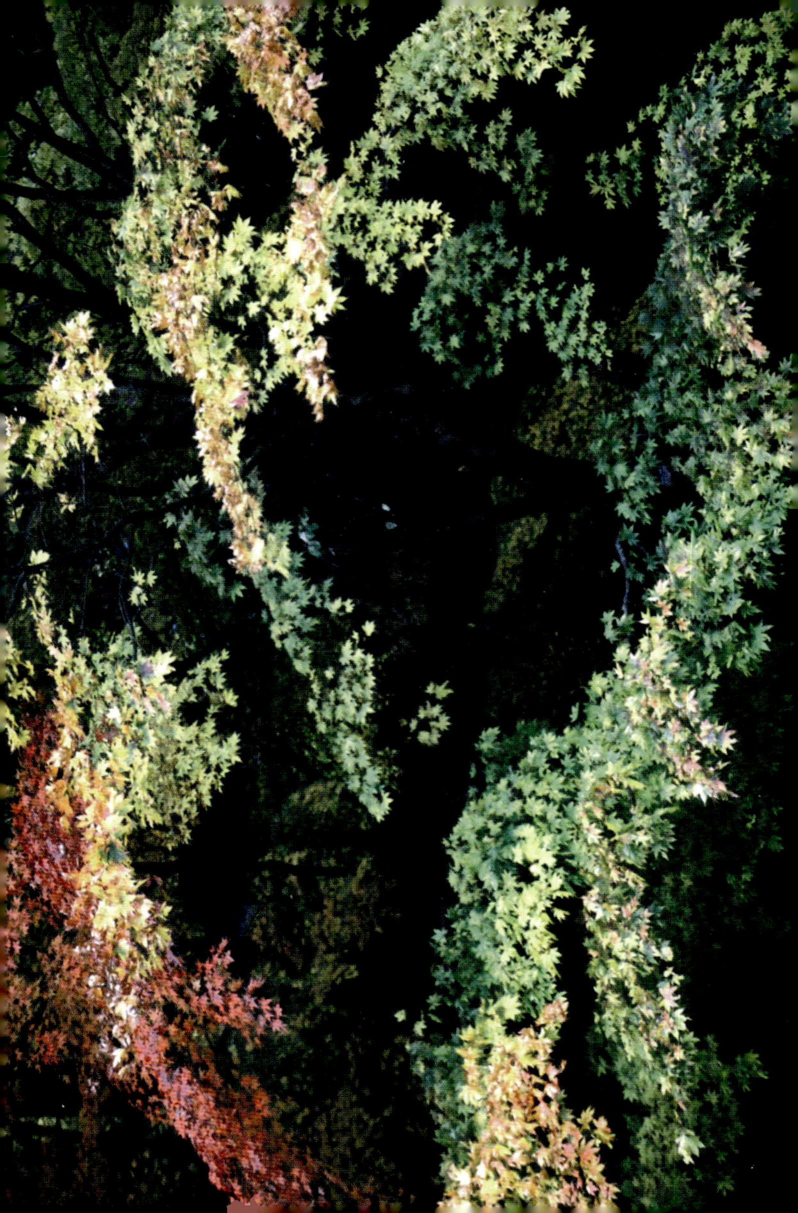

Maples in temperate forest, Japan *UNEP/Still Pictures*

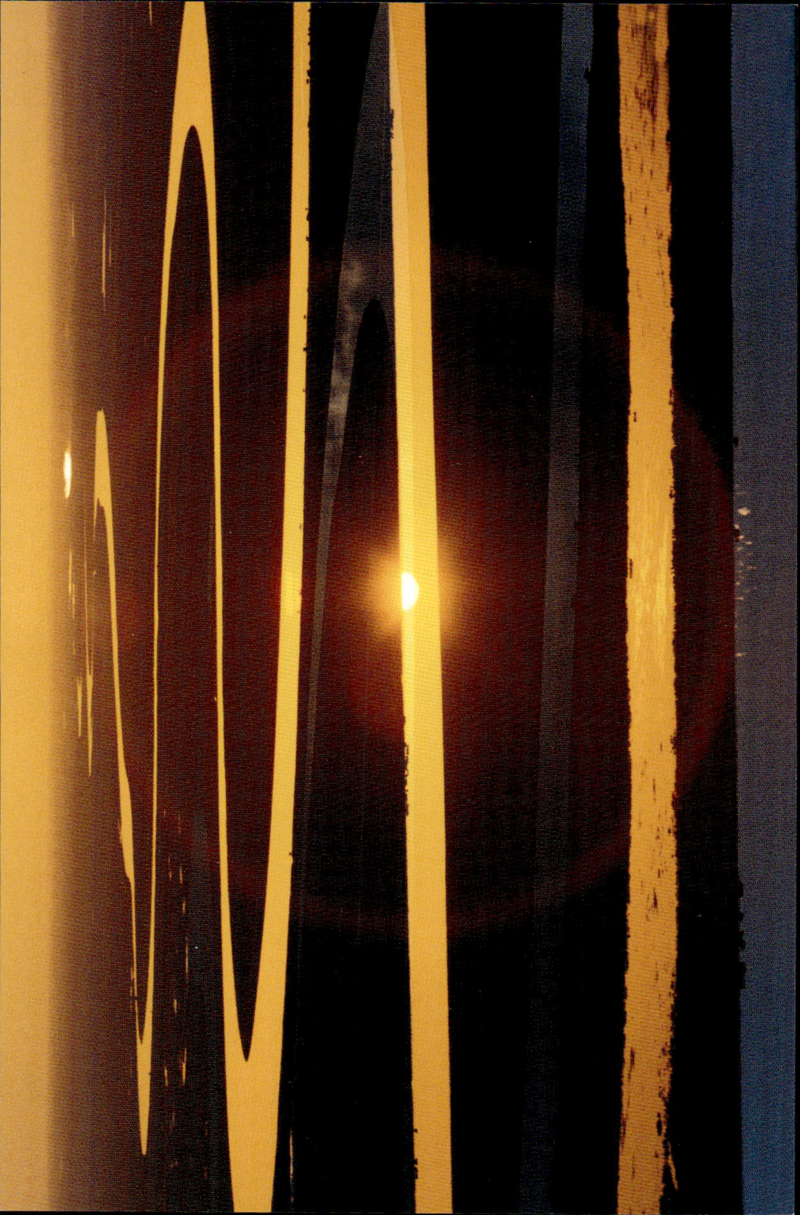

Sunset on river, China *UNEP/Still Pictures*

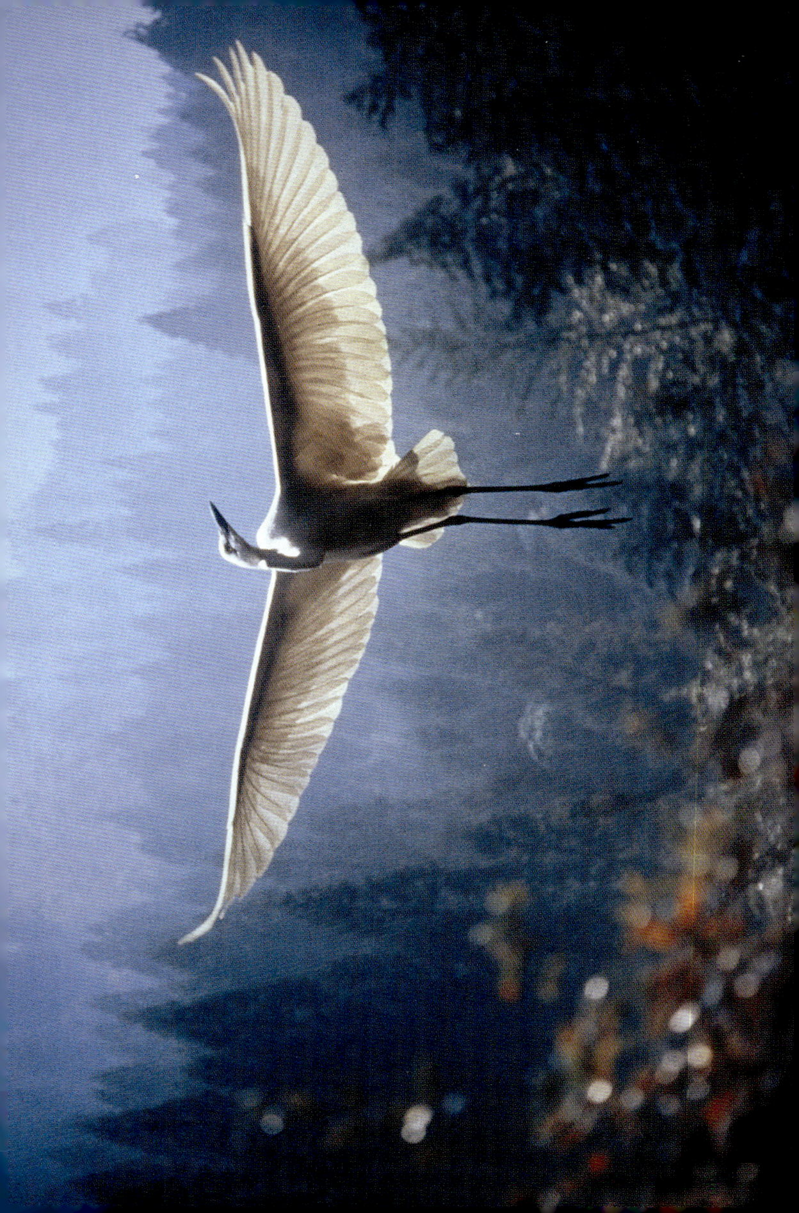

Egret, Japan *R Kawakami/UNEP/Still Pictures*

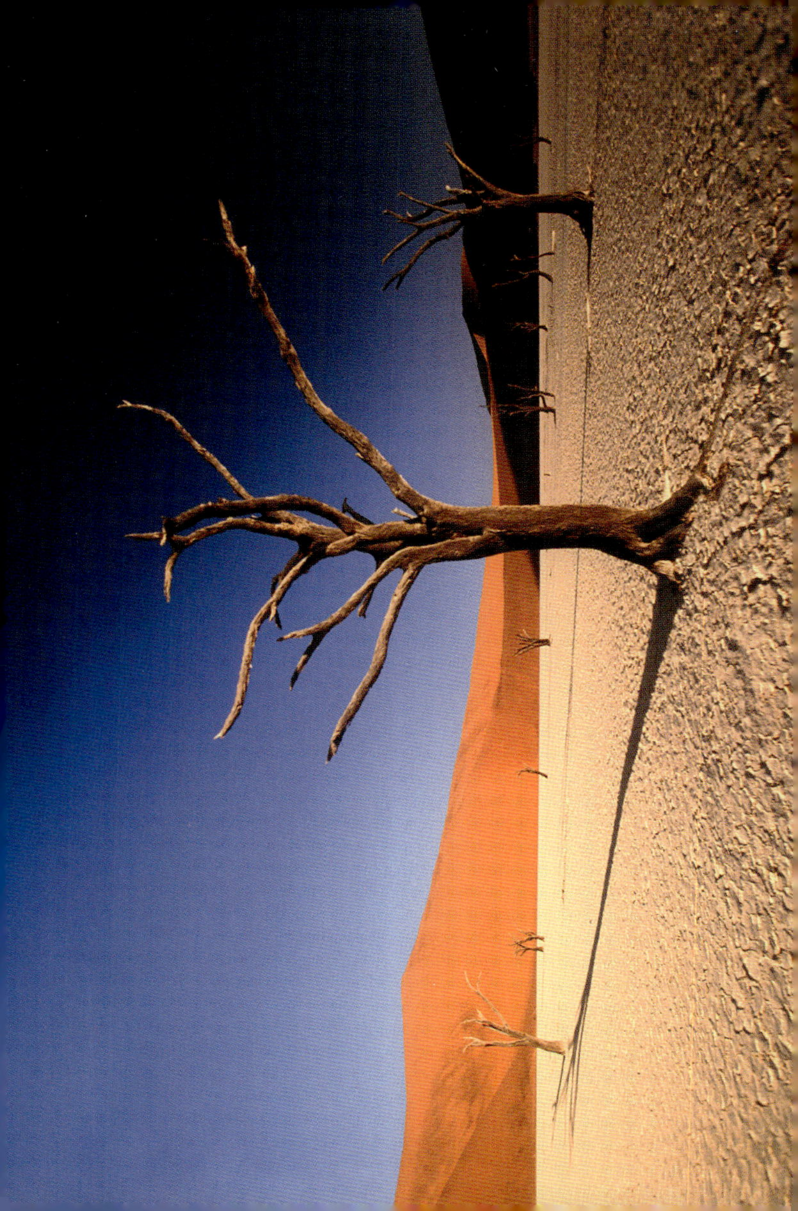

Dead trees, Namibia, Africa *Frans Lemmens/Still Pictures*

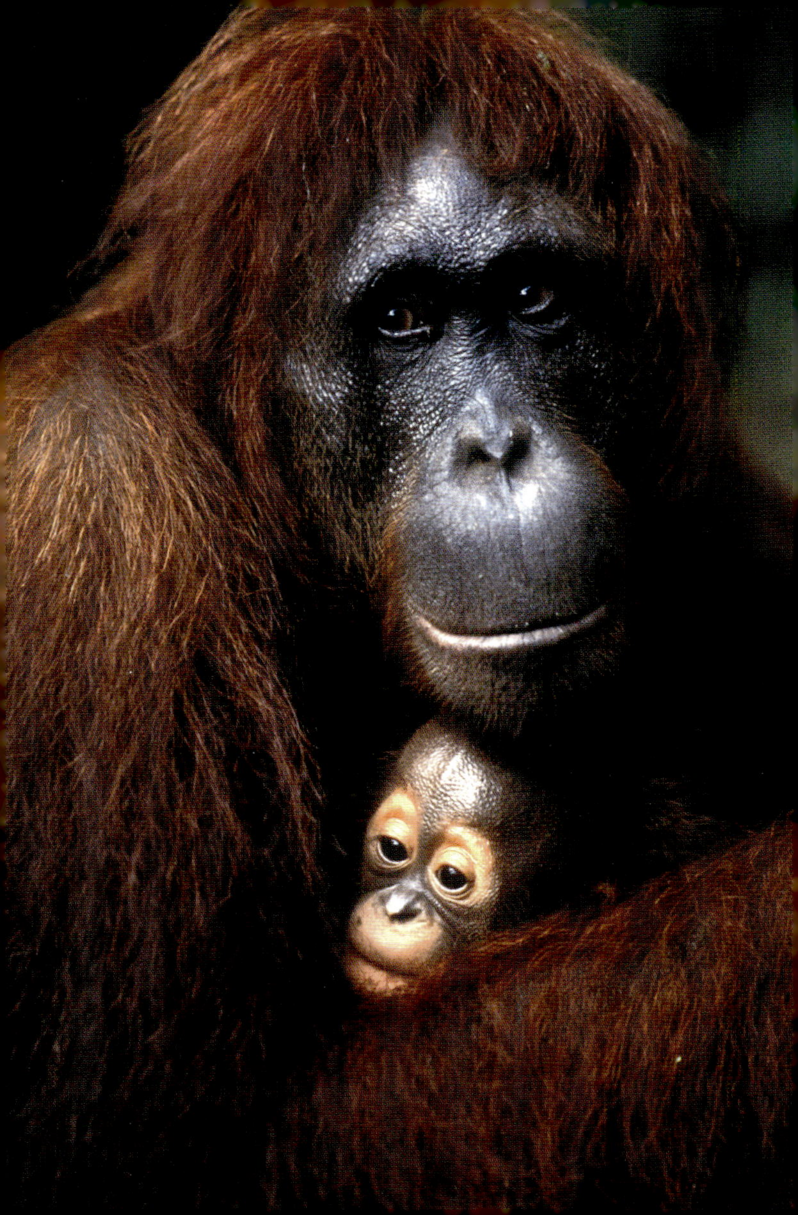

Orang-utans, Kalimantan, Indonesia *Cyril Ruoso/Still Pictures*

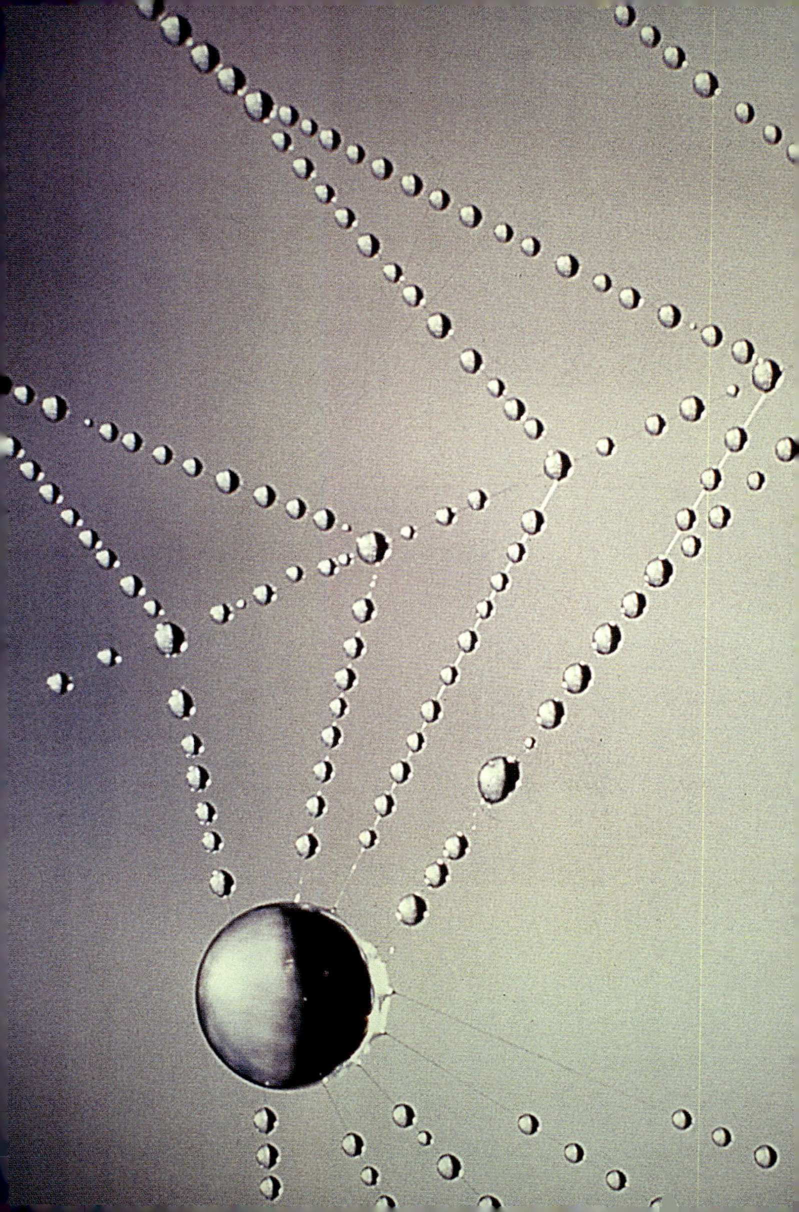

Dewdrop on web, California, USA *David Cavagnaro/Still Pictures*

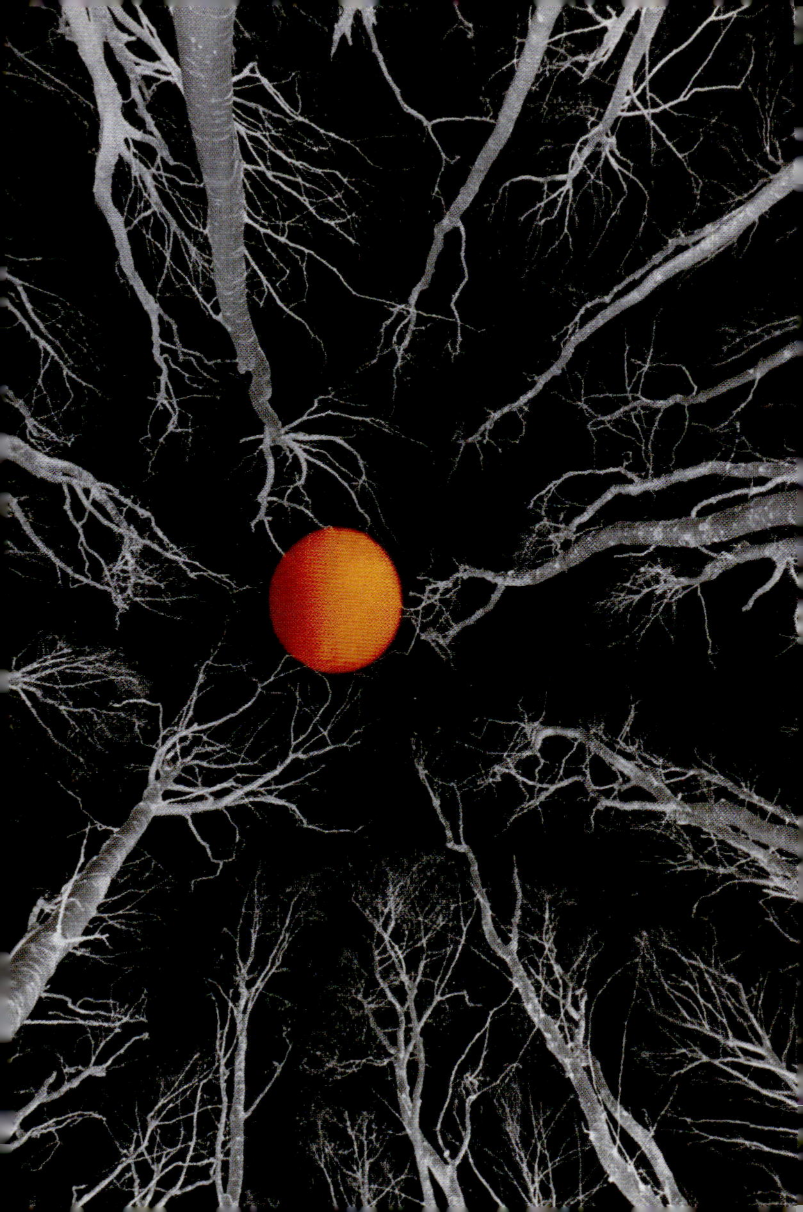

Sunrise in the forest *BEN/UNEP/Still Pictures*

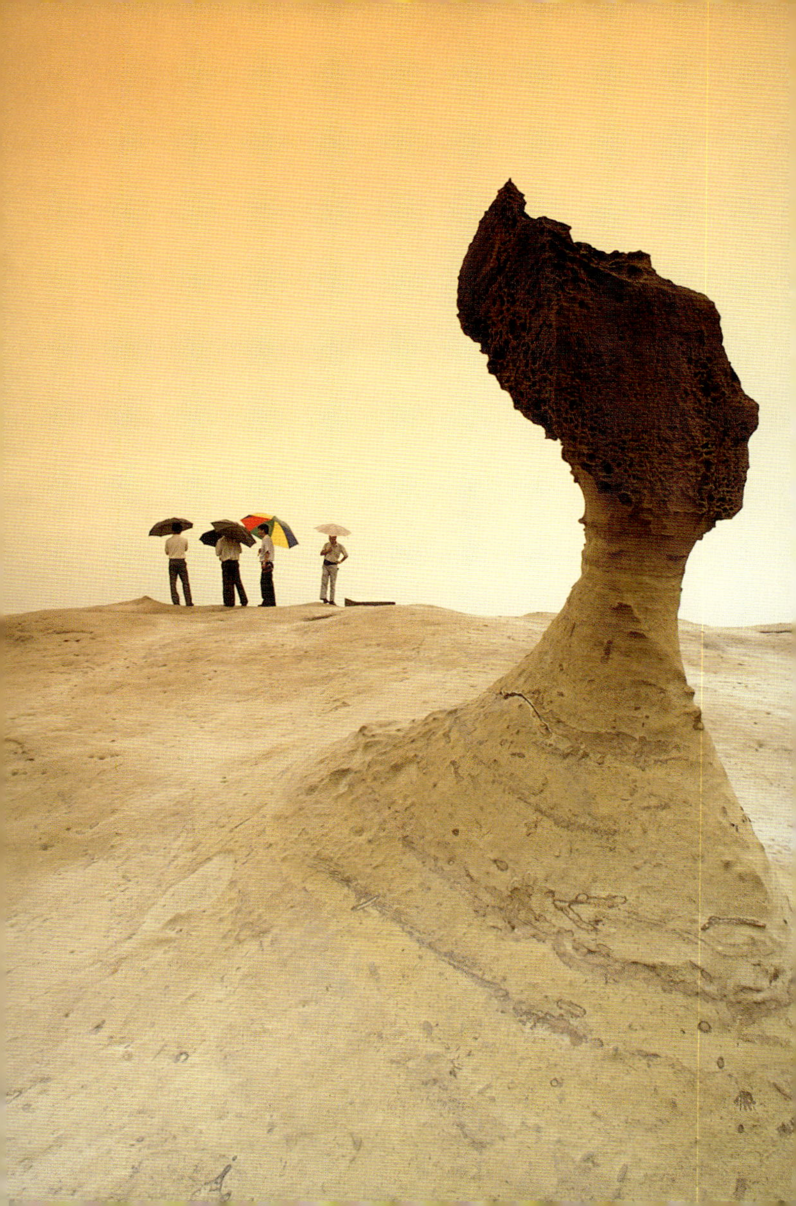

Queen's Head rock, Taiwan *Chris Stowers/Panos*

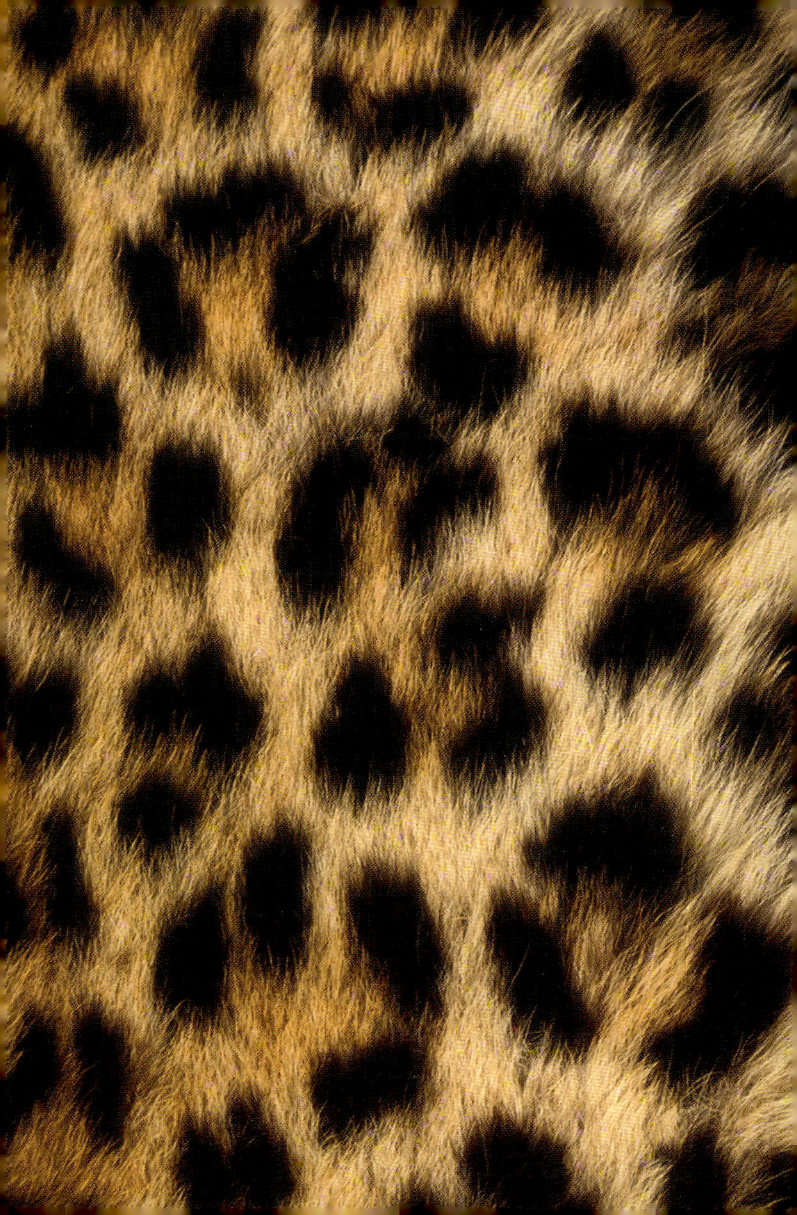

Leopard's fur, South Africa *Roger de la Harpe/Still Pictures*

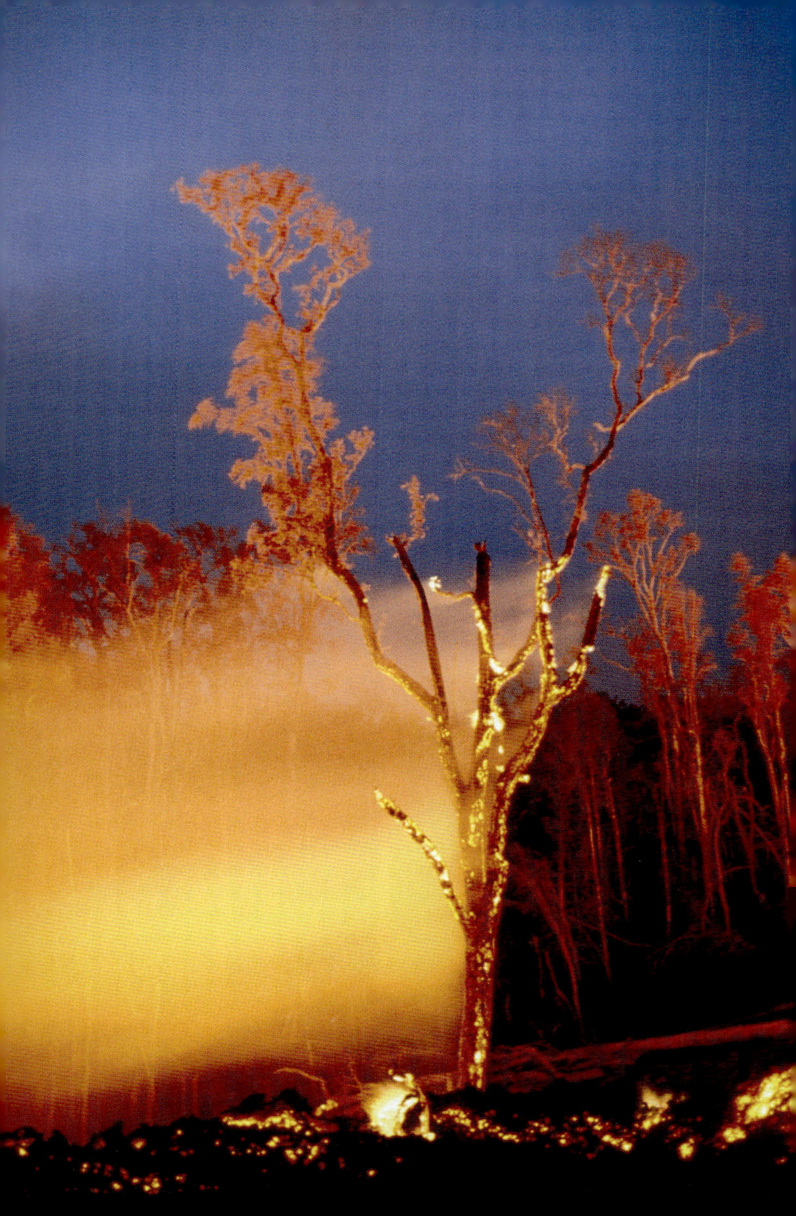

Lava igniting tree, Hawaii *S&D O'Meara/UNEP/Still Pictures*

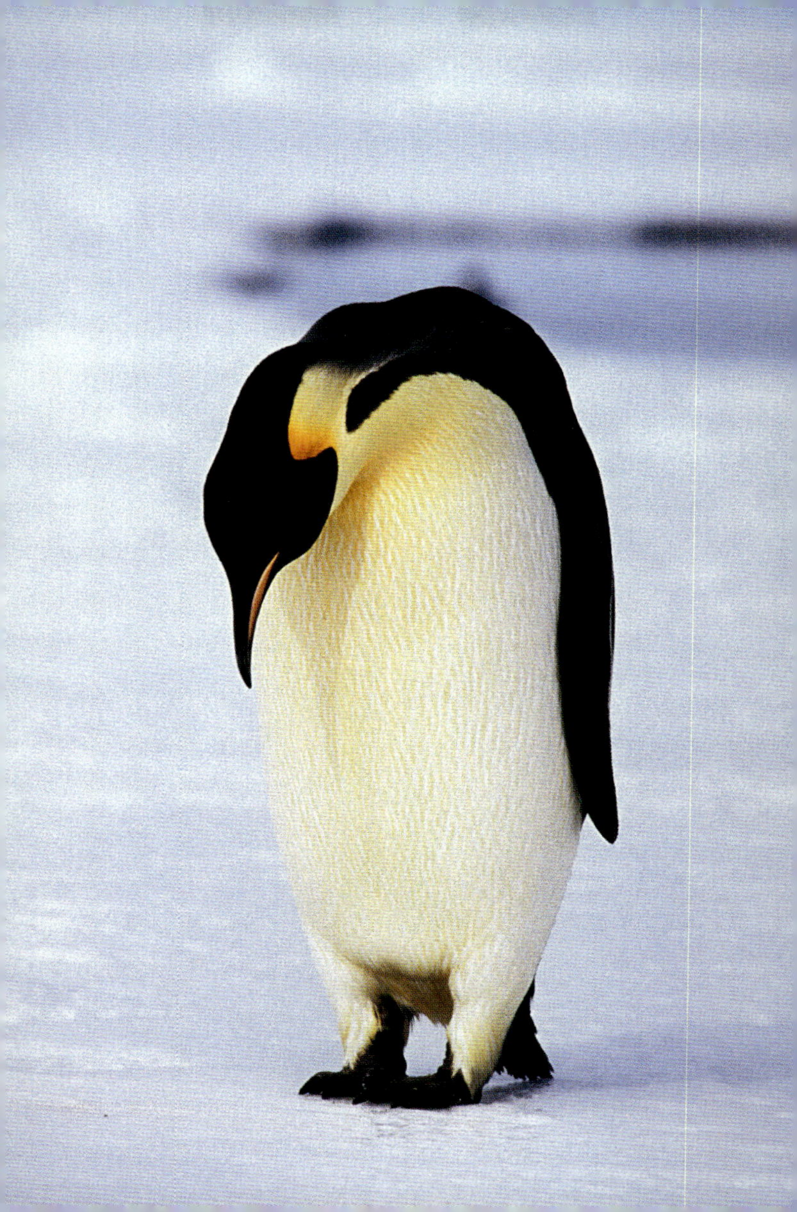

Penguin, Antarctica *Birnbau/UNEP/Still Pictures*

Other NI publications:

Our Fragile World – The beauty of a planet under pressure

By Troth Wells and Caspar Henderson

Celebrate the beauty of our world – and its diversity – through these wonderful photographs. Over 150 stunning images from the world's best photographers illustrate the many ways in which nature and human life share the planet – sometimes in balance, sometimes not. From nature's delicate coral reefs to the human-made ecosystem of rice paddies; from the horrible beauty of the ozone hole to the innocent delight of penguins, these photos celebrate the wonder of the world we have and cannot afford to lose. The compelling photos make you look twice, and think again. It's a beautiful, complex, fragile planet; we can adapt and learn, working with nature to protect it.

> 'This splendid book brings together the beauty of the earth and the shame of our insults.'
>
> James Lovelock, environmentalist and author of *The Gaia Theory*

Water, life force

By Maggie Black

This large-format, lavishly illustrated book is a celebration of water – its history and many roles in the human and natural world. Author Maggie Black delves into literary and folkloric sources for extracts and quotations that highlight and complement more than 100 photos demonstrating the majesty of water. Images range from oceans, rivers and snow-capped mountains to everyday scenes of people using water: planting seedlings, boiling kettles and watering animals. *Water, life force* also examines contemporary issues such as privatization, dams and pollution. The text and photos are interspersed with many droplets of facts.

Vanishing Footprints – Nomadic People Speak

By Ann Perry and Anthony Swift

This photography book captures the variety of nomadic cultures including the herders, hunters and foragers of Africa; the rainforest dwellers of the Amazon basin and the peoples of the snowbound areas in the Arctic Circle. In their own words, nomadic people tell of the ups and downs of their daily lives: herding, story-telling, hunting, worshipping, and confronting the impact of globalization. 120 full-colour photos give powerful visual insights into their lives.

The World Guide 10th Edition

An alternative reference to the countries of our planet

Researched and written in Uruguay, this essential reference work gives information on every country in the world plus data and information on health, education, food and special reports on topics such as HIV/AIDS, globalization, human rights and environmental issues. *The World Guide* provides a wealth of information and has a unique perspective as a reference work produced in the developing world.

For further details on the **New Internationalist** magazine, publications and other products please visit our website at **www.newint.org** or contact your nearest office:

United Kingdom and Europe
55 Rectory Road
Oxford OX4 1BW
Tel: +44 1865 811400
Email: ni@newint.org

Ireland
PO Box 8115
Dublin 15
Tel: +353 1 811 5970
Email: ni@dna.ie

Canada/US
401 Richmond Street West
Studio 393
Toronto
Ontario M5V 3A8
Tel: +1 416 588 6478
Email: nican@web.ca

Australia and PNG
28 Austin Street
Adelaide
SA 5000
Tel: +61 8 8232 1563
Email: helenp@newint.com.au

Aotearoa/New Zealand
PO Box 35038
Christchurch
Tel: +64 3 386 3153
Email: newint@chch.planet.org.nz